Castles and Cathedrals

The architecture of power
1066 – 1550

David Aldred

Head of History

Cleeve Comprehensive School

CAMBRIDGE
UNIVERSITY PRESS

Published by the Press Syndicate of the University of Cambridge
The Pitt Building, Trumpington Street, Cambridge CB2 1RP
40 West 20th Street, New York, NY 10011 - 4211, USA
10 Stamford Road, Oakleigh, Melbourne 3166, Australia

First published 1993

Printed in Great Britain at the University Press, Cambridge
A catalogue record for this book is available from the British Library

Notice to teachers
Many of the sources used in this book have been adapted or abridged from the original.

ISBN 0 521 42842 4

Credit and caption for Cover illustration: 'Chronique d'Angleterre', by permission of the British Library

Illustrations by Martin Salisbury, Sharon Pallent, Stephen Conlin, Maggie Brand, Caroline Bilson, Sue Shields, Martin Sanders

Picture research by Callie Kendall

Acknowledgements
4, Osterreichische Nationalbibliothek, Vienna; 5t, Dean and Chapter of Canterbury/photo by Ben May; 5b, 26, 28r, 31t, 34t, A.F. Kersting; 7, 17t, 27t, 29b, 31b, 32, 34b, 35t, 35b, 36l, 38, 42, Aerofilms; 9t, 30, The Bridgeman Art Library/ British Library, London; 9b, Bridgeman Art Library/Bibliothèque Nationale, Paris; 11l, 28l, 29t, 53b, Cadw: Welsh Historic Monuments, Crown Copyright; 11r, 20t, 25, 46, 47, reproduced by permission of the British Library; 21, Skyscan Balloon Photography; 17 inset, 54, 60t, © English Heritage; 27b, Royal Commission on the Ancient & Historical Monuments of Scotland; 33, English Life Publications, Limited; 36r, by courtesy of Dean and Chapter of Westminster; 37, Michael Jenner; 40, E.T. Archive/British Library; 43t, Lauros-Giraudon/ Archives Nationales, Paris; 43c, courtesy of Christopher de Hamel; 43b, © Bibliothèque Royale Albert 1er, Bruxelles; MS 9278-80, f. 1049t, reproduced by courtesy of the Trustees of the British Museum; 49c, 50, E.T. Archive/Victoria & Albert Museum; 51, English Heritage/ Terry Ball; 52, Bridgeman Art Library/City of Bristol Museum & Art Gallery; 53t, National Portrait Gallery, London; 55, reproduced by permission of the Syndics of the Fitzwilliam Museum, Cambridge; 57, West Air Photography; 60b, English Heritage/drawing by Terry Ball

Contents

Henry Yeveley:

the king's master mason

This book will help you to understand medieval castles, cathedrals and monasteries. They are great monuments to an age very different from our own. By studying them now we can learn a great deal about people who lived over five hundred years ago.

Who built the castles, cathedrals and monasteries of medieval Britain?

Building in the image of God

Many different people were involved in building medieval castles and cathedrals, but without the architect nothing could have happened. His genius conquered the problems of design and construction. A castle had to be a fortress and a home; cathedrals and monasteries had to soar up to the sky, look beautiful but be strong. The architect had to understand geometry. He had to be able to find and organise the workforce of masons, carpenters, smiths, glaziers and all the other craftsmen and their labourers. In his work people believed he reflected the work of God, the Great Architect, who had designed the world.

SOURCE A

Architects were important in the Middle Ages because people believed they were copying the work of God, who had created the world. This picture shows God as an architect designing the world.
From an Old Testament written in France, about 1250.

Henry Yeveley

We know the names of nearly 2,000 British architects who lived between 1050 and 1550 but the most famous was probably Henry Yeveley from Staffordshire.

Born in about 1325, he rose from being the son of a humble stone mason earning ten shillings (50p) a month, to become 'the Master Mason of the King's Works throughout England', earning over £3,000 each year. When he died in 1400 he owned many houses in London, and even a brewery!

Henry Yeveley learnt his craft in Staffordshire but, because of the shortage of craftsmen after the Black Death, he – like many other masons – made his way to London to seek his fortune. Unlike most of the others, however, he was successful. In 1360 he was working for King Edward III on the Palace of Westminster and the Tower of London. Later he worked on old St Paul's Cathedral and when Richard II died in 1399, it was Henry Yeveley who was asked to design the King's tomb.

Although architects like Henry Yeveley needed rich patrons to provide the huge sums of money which such buildings cost, the architects were the creators who designed the work and we can still admire their achievements today.

SOURCE D

One of Henry's greatest works was the western part of the nave of Westminster Abbey, which is visited by millions of people every year.

SOURCE B

This carving in Canterbury Cathedral cloisters is thought to be of Henry Yeveley.

SOURCE C

Not everyone felt that architects or master masons should be respected.

'Master masons with a rod and gloves in their hands say to others "cut it for me this way" and work not themselves but take higher pay.'

From a sermon by Nicholas de Biard, 1261

- Why do you think some people did not like master masons or architects?

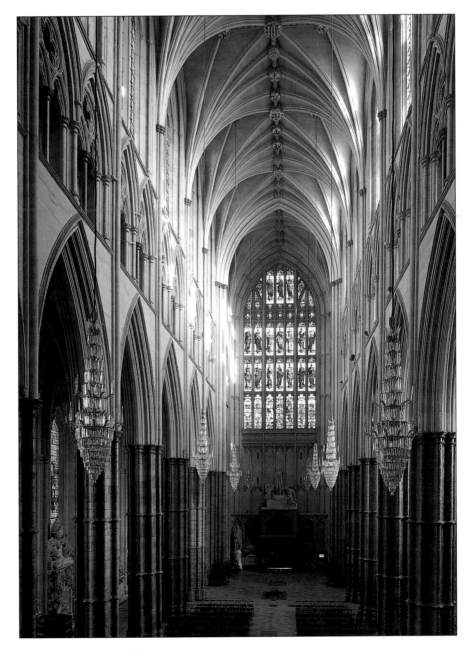

Monuments to feudalism

Castles and cathedrals represent power and authority. They were built by people at the top of the feudal system, which you will have learned about in your study of medieval Britain. Many castles still exist today even though most medieval buildings have disappeared.

Who had the wealth to build them?

Castles were introduced to Britain by the Normans. They were private strongholds, built by kings or powerful landholders to protect themselves and their families while they ruled their lands.

A cathedral was a church containing the chair, or *cathedra*, of a bishop. It was built for the worship of God, for saying prayers and as the place from which the bishop ruled his bishopric or diocese. Twenty cathedrals already existed in 1066.

Power and wealth

In Roman and Anglo-Saxon times fortifications had been built around communities not individual families. After the Norman conquest, castles and cathedrals towered over the surrounding countryside as signs of the power of kings, lords and bishops. They were the patrons who had the wealth to hire architects like Henry Yeveley to build such magnificent designs. The poor peasants and townspeople, who worked for the lords and made them rich, have no such monuments to their lives.

SOURCE A

King William was a very good example of a rich and powerful lord who built castles, cathedrals and monasteries.

'1068: When the King was told that the people in the north had rebelled against him, he marched to Nottingham and built a castle there, and so on to York, and there built two castles, and also in Lincoln.

1087: On the very spot where God granted him the conquest of England he built a great abbey, and put monks in it and gave it rich gifts. During his reign the great cathedral at Canterbury was built and many another throughout England.'

The Anglo-Saxon Chronicle

---

1 Why did people build castles and cathedrals in the Middle Ages? Why were both castles and cathedrals often built by the same powerful people?

2 Do you think we can get a clear picture of life in the Middle Ages if we only study castles and cathedrals? Explain your answer.

SOURCE B

William the Conqueror made the Bishop of Durham ruler over the northern lands on the borders of Scotland. By 1100 his castle and cathedral were already in existence. This aerial photograph shows how close together the castle and cathedral are at Durham.

● *Why do you think this site was chosen?*

Building castles and cathedrals

Castles and cathedrals were the largest buildings of the Middle Ages. Large numbers of workmen using only muscle power and simple machinery toiled over long periods of time to create strong fortresses and beautiful churches.

How were the castles and cathedrals built?

The planning

Castles and cathedrals were carefully planned by architects using their own experience and perhaps helped by handwritten books of designs. They first drew a plan on parchment or on the ground and some architects made models of churches.

It was important to choose a good site. Castles needed a dominant position and solid foundations. Most cathedrals were built on the site of earlier churches because these were already holy places. First the site had to be levelled. Then, by using geometry, the plan was marked out on the ground and the foundations were dug. In soft ground, wooden posts were driven into the ground so that the walls had a good base. Stones were poured in for the foundations and only then did the walls rise out of the ground.

A modern drawing showing the building of a medieval castle.

● *Which activities can you also find in Sources A and B?*

The cost of building

The main problems facing the architects were hiring a workforce and obtaining building materials. This is where most of the money was spent and, as castles and cathedrals became larger and more elaborate during the Middle Ages, fewer and fewer people could afford to pay for them. Hundreds of small motte-and-bailey castles were built by the Norman lords shortly after 1066 but 450 years later only Henry VIII could afford to build new castles. No new cathedral was started after 1350 and none was even being rebuilt by 1550.

SOURCE A ▶

This illustration, made in about 1430, shows the Bible story of the building of the Tower of Babel with the angels striking the builders as they build towards heaven.

- *Make a list of all the different activities shown in Sources A and B.*
- *Why do you think that the artist has shown the king and architect as larger than the workers?*

The workforce

This needed great organisation. So many people were needed they often came from all over Britain. The architect usually had to rely on the master craftsmen – the masons, carpenters and smiths – to find their own skilled workers.

The workers stopped work frequently. Little work was done on Sundays and religious feast days or during most of the winter. But no work meant no pay, as you can work out from the Dover Castle accounts in Source C. Wages increased after the Black Death, but no craftsman could earn the fees that architects like Henry Yeveley demanded.

SOURCE B

A medieval painting showing the construction of a cathedral in France.

- What can you learn from these accounts about the pay of the different workmen and the number of days they worked?

Barrels of money

Paying wages to large numbers of workers caused problems. At the end of the thirteenth century, one and a half million silver pennies were sent in barrels to pay six months' wages to the workers at Beaumaris Castle in north Wales – paid for by taxes demanded by King Edward I.

The materials

The Normans first built castles in wood but by the year 1100 stone castles were becoming more common. Cathedrals were always built of stone. Huge quantities were needed. Most stone was local but some stone was taken long distances because it was special – marble from Purbeck in Dorset, high-quality limestone from Caen in Normandy. Transport was a problem. In 1237 stone which cost 3s (15p) at the quarry in Bath cost 22s (110p) to carry to Marlborough thirty miles away.

- Who was to blame for this disaster?

But stone was not the only material needed. Vast quantities of sand, lime and water were needed for the mortar; timber was needed for floors and ceilings, for doors, shutters and lavatory seats; lead was needed for roofs; iron and steel for nails, hinges and firegrates; walls were plastered and painted; cathedral windows needed glass.

Was the building always successful?

Many medieval castles and cathedrals are still standing today but the builders were not always successful. Things sometimes went badly wrong. On the night of 19 October 1360 a tremendous gale blew down the nave of Edward III's abbey at Vale Royal in Cheshire. It had taken a century to build! Nothing now remains of such accidents and we would know nothing about them if the events had not been recorded for us by the chroniclers.

SOURCE E

Master James of St George was another great architect. He was hired by King Edward I to build his castles in north Wales. He came from Savoy in southern France and brought new ideas with him, such as spiral scaffolding. The holes can still be seen at Conwy Castle.

SOURCE F

This medieval painting shows how spiral scaffolding was used.

How long did the building take?

It is difficult to answer this question because building and rebuilding continued for years. Castles could be built quickly – Conwy Castle in north Wales was built in five summers (1283–87) – but the mixed architectural styles of cathedrals tell us they were often rebuilt several times between 1066 and 1500. Generations of monks at Canterbury or Chester lived on building sites and work was constantly interrupted by their services!

---

1 Design a flow chart using five boxes like the ones in the diagram. Choose a label for each of the middle boxes and write a short paragraph in each box to explain three stages of building between planning and completion. Compare your flow chart with your neighbour's. After discussion draw another flow chart to incorporate all your ideas. How many boxes do you have now?

| Planning | → | | → | | → | | → | Completion |

2 How useful are the sources in this chapter for a historian investigating how the medieval builders worked? Copy this table into your book and complete it. Which source would you say is the most useful and why?

	Source letter	Uses for the historian	Problems in using the source
Modern drawing			
Medieval drawing			
Medieval chronicles			
Medieval accounts			
Physical remains			

The rise and

1066 –1087

The first type of castle was the motte-and-bailey castle. A wooden tower stood on a motte – a steep-sided mound of earth – and looked down on a bailey. The bailey was a level area protected by a ditch and a bank with a fence on top. The wooden tower was relatively safe but there was very little living space inside it. By 1087 William also had castles with stone towers, or keeps, in Colchester, Exeter and London.

1087–1154

Stone castles now became more common. Mottes could not support square stone keeps and most were abandoned. If the motte was kept, the wooden wall on top of the mound was replaced by a stone wall known as a shell keep. The stone walls of the keep provided greater safety and bailey walls were heightened to protect against the battering ram and siege tower – ideas brought back from the First Crusade in 1096.

1154 –1216

Keeps were strengthened further by having rounded corners or being built completely round, to prevent the battering or undermining of their weakest parts. When the bailey fence was built of stone it was called a curtain wall. As the bailey defences became stronger, there was less need for the motte or the keep to protect the people in the castle. However, motte-and-bailey castles were still being built by the English in Ireland around 1171 when Henry II tried to conquer that country. Historians have calculated there were 327 castles in England by 1216.

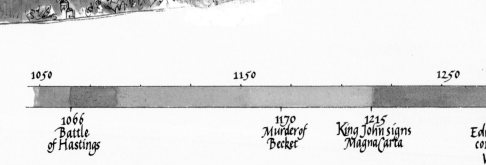

| 1050 | 1150 | 1250 |

1066
Battle
of Hastings

1170
Murder of
Becket

1215
King John signs
Magna Carta

1284
Edward I
conquers
Wales

fall of the castle

1216 –1277

Designers concentrated on improving the defences of existing castles. Gateways were protected by drawbridges, portcullises and heavy doors. Sections of the top of the castle walls, called machicolations, jutted out. There were holes in the floors of these sections through which the defenders could fire or drop things on their attackers. Wall towers were better designed. They became rounded so the defenders had an even better field of fire. Sometimes the towers could be defended even if the rest of the castle had fallen.

1277–1330

The most sophisticated of all castles were built in north Wales after Edward I defeated the Welsh princes in 1277 and 1282. Caernarfon and Conwy had high walls, rounded towers and strong gate-houses. Concentric castles were encircled by more than one wall, the inner walls being higher than the outer walls. Both walls had towers from which defenders could fire. The men on the inner walls fired over the heads of the soldiers on the outer wall. This meant that attackers had to break through two walls, all the time being fired on from all angles.

1330–1550

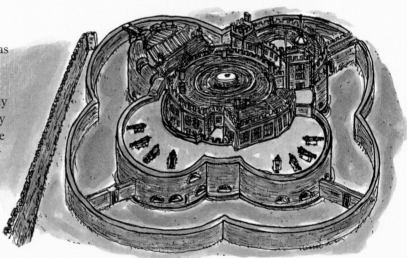

Even before the first cannon had been invented, the castle was no longer needed so much. Comfort had become more important to the people living in the castle as the times had become less violent. Some castles were built as fortified stately homes but few people could actually afford to build castles by this time. In 1538 Henry VIII feared a French invasion. The castles built on the south coast were the last to be built. They were forts rather than homes.

1350   1450   1550

314
nglish defeated
Bannockburn

1381
Peasants
Revolt

1485
Richard III killed
at Bosworth

Changing castle styles

Most castles were altered several times during the Middle Ages. Kings and barons were always trying to impress other people, and would rebuild in the latest style to protect against new weapons of attack. It is possible to use the different styles of architecture to work out when castles were changed. Plans of castles are also useful.

What can the architecture and plan of a castle tell us about how it was changed in the past?

Chepstow Castle is a very good example of a castle that has been changed several times since it was first built. It stands on a cliff looking down on the River Wye on the border of England and Wales.

Phase 3 – windows added to the great hall

Phase 1 – doorway to the great hall

Phase 2 – round towers added to east curtain wall

Phase 6 – musket openings in the south wall

SOURCE A
Chepstow Castle as it appears today.

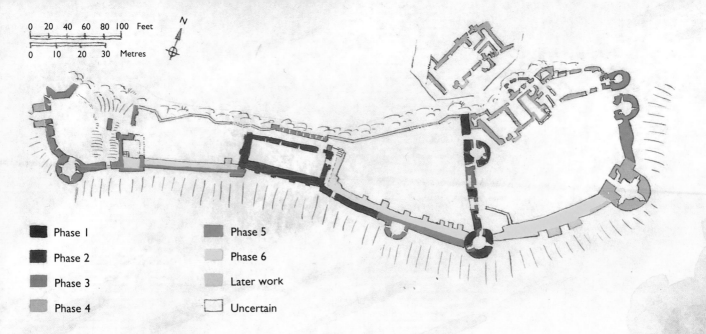

Phase 1 ■

Phase 2 ■

Phase 3 ■

Phase 4 ■

Phase 5 ■

Phase 6 ■

Later work ■

Uncertain ▭

SOURCE B

The ground plan of Chepstow Castle.

● *Use tracing paper to draw the plan of Phase 3. What problems do you meet?*

---

1 Draw a timeline for the years 1067–2000. Mark on the six phases. For each phase draw a small sketch of a feature of the castle dating from that phase.

2 The periods when Chepstow changed were far shorter than the periods when no changes took place and the castle simply remained as it was. Were the changes more important?

3 Mark on your timeline when Chepstow Castle stopped changing for the better and started to change for the worse. Does the whole class agree on a date?

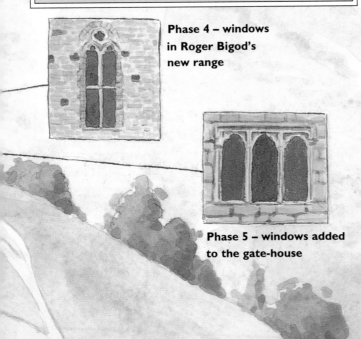

Phase 4 – windows in Roger Bigod's new range

Phase 5 – windows added to the gate-house

Phase 1 1067–1075

The first castle was built by one of William's knights, William Fitz Osbern, as a base for the Normans to conquer south Wales. He built the parts we now call the Great Tower, or keep, and the upper and middle baileys.

Phase 2 about 1200

Two towers were added by a new owner – a powerful baron called William Marshal. Use the plan to work out where they were built.

Phase 3 1219–1245

William had five sons who changed the castle again. They added another storey to the keep and increased the area of the castle. What else did they add to the castle?

Phase 4 1270–1300

None of William's sons had any children and so the castle passed through William's daughter to Roger Bigod, Earl of Norfolk, an adviser to King Edward I. He built a fine new block of rooms in the lower bailey and turned Marten's Tower into his own private castle within the castle.

Phase 5 1525–1550

There was little change until the Tudor period when the large household of the Earls of Worcester lived here. New windows were put into the gate-house and houses were built along the east curtain wall.

Phase 6 1640–1660

Cromwell's armies twice captured Chepstow easily in the Civil War. The south wall was thickened against cannon-balls, and openings for muskets were made, but the castle was never attacked again.

The castle gradually crumbled away although people lived in parts of it until the 1950s when it was given to the government as a historic monument.

4 'The bones of the kingdom'

When you visit a castle you can gain some idea from its position why it was built on that particular spot, but just examining the site will not tell you very much about the need for the castle in the first place. In the twelfth century William of Newburgh called the royal castles 'the bones of the kingdom'.

Why were castles built?

Symbols of power and authority

Castles were built by rulers: kings and queens, barons, bishops and knights. They were built to dominate town and country so their owners could literally look down on the common people, who were thus always reminded of their lowly place in the feudal system. Today's ruins were once alive as signs of the power and authority of the few over the powerlessness of the many.

Royal castles

Royal castles were built to defend kingdoms. When William the Conqueror built the first castles they defended England against attack from Scotland and the north; when Henry VIII built the last castles, they defended England against attack from France in the south. Royal castles were also used to control the monarch's lands and as places to stay on their journeys through their kingdom. In 1214 there were 93 royal castles.

Baronial castles

Other castles were built by barons and knights; some were built by bishops. They were built in the same way as the royal castles and they were usually built to control the lords' estates. The owners stayed in them as they travelled round their lands. In 1214 there were 179 baronial castles.

The importance of the site

The site was carefully chosen so the owner could impress as well as defend. Hilltops were ideal places but good sites could be created artificially, by mottes, ditches and moats, particularly where castles were built in towns. Remember the houses and shops around the site would have looked very different in the Middle Ages compared to today.

Beeston Castle, Cheshire – a case study

Ranulf, Earl of Chester, was a very powerful baron who not only held the whole of the county of Cheshire for the king, but had land in fifteen other counties and held twenty-three castles. His main castle was at Chester, from where he was supposed to protect England against attacks from Wales.

He fought many skirmishes with the Welsh prince, Llywelyn the Great, until they signed a treaty in 1218. Two years later Ranulf went to Egypt on a Crusade. In 1225, after his return, he started building Beeston Castle on an isolated hill fifteen miles from Chester. He planned it with a huge outer bailey nearly surrounding the inner bailey as he had seen on the Crusades. He planned very few buildings inside the inner bailey but there was plenty of space for soldiers to camp within the walls. He never quite finished it, and when his son died in 1237 it passed to King Henry III, who used it in his campaign against the Welsh as fighting had again broken out.

SOURCE A

Beeston Castle commands a high position looking across the flat plains into Wales.

SOURCE B ▶

An artist's drawing of Beeston Castle in 1265 when we know royal soldiers camped there.

1 Why was Beeston Castle built? To answer this question, copy and complete the table below using the information and sources in the case study.

2 What can we learn from the example of Beeston about why castles were built? Was it just because it had a good site?

	Yes	No
As Earl Ranulf's home		
To run his estates		
As a garrison for soldiers		
To keep the Welsh out of England		
As a base to attack the Welsh		
To guard tracks into Wales		
To experiment with new ideas in castle building brought from the Crusades		
To show people he was rich and powerful		
Because the hill gave good protection		

5 Keys to the land

Castles were built to protect people and their property. If opponents wanted to destroy the owner's power and authority, and take the land, the castle had to be captured. Attackers used a number of different methods.

What happened when a castle was attacked?

The castle as a stronghold

The development of the castle was closely linked to changing methods of attack. Designers of castles were always looking for new ways of making life difficult for would-be attackers.

The attack

There were two main methods of attacking castles: batter down the defences, or besiege the site until the defenders gave in. When battering the defences the attackers used a variety of siege engines.

● Can you work out from the illustration how each one was used?

Belfry

Ballista

Battering ram

Mangonel

Castles could be attacked in other ways:

- Mining involved tunnelling under a wall so that it would collapse. You can still see a mine of 1547 at St Andrew's Castle in Scotland, where the defenders successfully countermined and drove out the attackers.

- Diseased animal carcasses were hurled into castles to spread diseases; heads from prisoners were sometimes hurled in to demoralise defenders. Occasionally attackers successfully climbed up the lavatory chutes.

- From 1326 cannon were used but they were not reliable. In 1460 King James II of Scotland was killed when his own cannon blew up whilst attacking Roxburgh Castle in Northumberland.

Which side was successful?

Sometimes the defenders were successful and sometimes the attackers. Defenders had the advantage of strong walls and towers from which they could fire down on their attackers. Defensive features such as the barbican, which crowded attackers into a small space under concentrated fire, and machicolations made the assault on the castle even more hazardous for the attackers. Sieges sometimes failed because the attackers could not afford to pay for the wages, food and supplies of their army but in the end any castle would fall if the siege was long enough. In 1266 Kenilworth Castle in Warwickshire fell to King Henry III, who had been able to afford a six-month siege.

Machicolations

Concentric walls

A modern artist's impression of an attack on a medieval castle.

The Siege of Dover Castle in 1216 – a case study

Even after Magna Carta in 1215, fighting continued between King John and some of his barons. The barons invited Prince Louis of France to be king of England, and in May 1216 he landed in England with an army of several thousand men. He immediately attacked Dover Castle, which was defended for King John by the Constable, Hubert de Burgh, with only one thousand soldiers.

SOURCE A

An imaginary siege drawn in the early fourteenth century.

● *How many different methods of fighting can you spot?*

SOURCE B

An artist's drawing showing what Dover Castle might have looked like in about 1200.

● *Use this drawing to work out the methods Prince Louis might have used in his attack.*

20

This is a description of the actual attack on Dover Castle by Prince Louis and his men.

'Louis, with a powerful force of French knights and soldiers, laid siege to Dover castle. He brought a mangonel and other siege engines in front of the castle, and began to batter the walls continuously; but Hugh de Burgh, a brave knight with a hundred and forty knights and a large number of soldiers who were defending the castle, destroyed many of the enemy until the French retreated further from the castle. At this Louis was greatly angered and swore he would not leave the place until the castle was taken and the garrison hung. Therefore, to fill them with terror, the French built a number of shops and other buildings in front of the main entrance to the castle so that the place looked like a market, for they hoped that they could force them to surrender by hunger and siege, as they could not defeat them by weapons. When Louis heard of the death of King John he was greatly pleased, as he confidently expected he now had the Kingdom of England in his own power. He summoned Hugh de Burgh, constable of Dover castle, to a conference and said to him, "Your lord King John is dead and you cannot hold this castle against me for long, therefore give it up and become faithful to me and I will give you many honours". To this offer Hugh is said to have replied, "Although my lord is dead he has sons and daughters to succeed him. As to surrendering the castle I will discuss it with my fellow knights". He then returned to the castle and told his friends who all refused to surrender in case they were charged with treason for so cowardly a surrender. When this was announced to Louis he decided to go to attack the weaker castles in the kingdom, leaving the strongest till they had been captured.'

Roger of Wendover, *Flowers of History*, about 1230

Dover Castle today. After the siege of 1216 the castle was strengthened by the addition of 'beaked' towers and strongly fortified entrances. The gate which the French had undermined was blocked by a new tower and protected by a large earthwork, known as the spur, and another tower which was placed in the moat.

1 How did Louis first attack Dover Castle? What did he do when this failed?

2 How did Louis try to use the death of King John to make the castle surrender? What did he do when this did not work?

3 Do you think the remains of the castle, which still exist, or the description by Roger of Wendover are more useful in helping you to understand the siege of 1216?

4 Why should you try to use both written descriptions and the remains of castles when trying to understand what happened in sieges?

6

Life in the castle

When people visit castles today, only echoes resound around the roofless walls, towers and empty kitchens, but once castles were alive with the sounds of people living their daily lives in the security of the stronghold. We need to use our imaginations carefully to re-create life in the castle.

What was life like for people who lived and worked in a medieval castle?

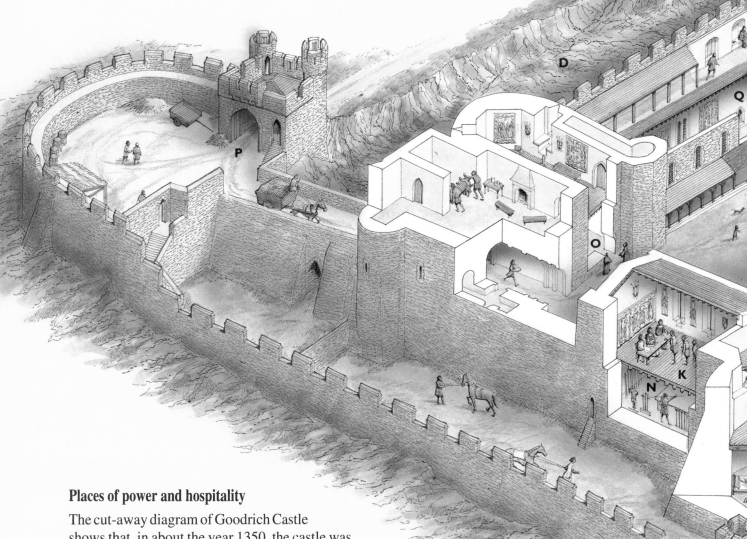

Places of power and hospitality

The cut-away diagram of Goodrich Castle shows that, in about the year 1350, the castle was a community of different households who lived in various parts of the building. The picture of life 250 years earlier would have been very different, for then the important rooms were all in the keep. During the Middle Ages castles became not only better protected but also more comfortable to live in.

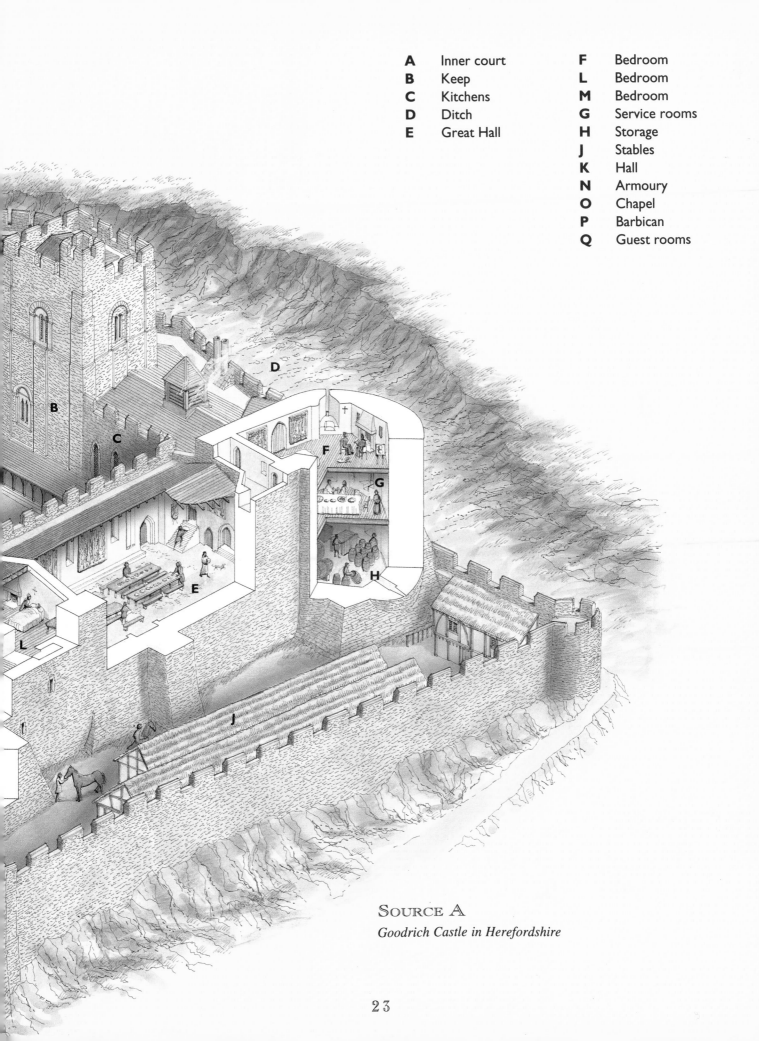

A	Inner court	F	Bedroom
B	Keep	L	Bedroom
C	Kitchens	M	Bedroom
D	Ditch	G	Service rooms
E	Great Hall	H	Storage
		J	Stables
		K	Hall
		N	Armoury
		O	Chapel
		P	Barbican
		Q	Guest rooms

SOURCE A

Goodrich Castle in Herefordshire

23

Who lived in castles?

The only people who lived permanently in a castle were servants under the constable. The castle owners travelled around their different castles, staying only for short periods until the food and drink available locally had been used up. When they arrived great preparations were needed. They brought many people and their own furniture – trestle-tables, benches, chairs, chests and linen, beds and bedding.

Dinner time

People often imagine that nobles spent all day feasting. This is not totally accurate, but dinner was a very important meal which started in late morning and sometimes lasted several hours. The only other regular meal was a light supper before bed.

Dinner was important because it was a chance for the lord to show how important he was. Here guests were well fed and entertained. The hall was alive with bustle and noise, warmth and welcome.

What did people do during the day?

Lords and ladies spent much of the day instructing their servants and entertaining guests. The lord or his steward also held courts to collect rents and punish criminals. In summer and winter they sometimes hunted deer and wild boar. Occasionally the castle grounds came alive with the colour and noise of a tournament.

If they had time, ladies embroidered. Children played with toys made of wood or with their pets – dogs and cats, or perhaps monkeys and magpies. Officials and servants spent their day making sure the castle was running smoothly. Preparing dinner was an important part of this. Most food was boiled or baked in the kitchen using an open fireplace and oven. This was often a long way from the halls where it was served.

Source B

Bartholomew the Englishman wrote an encyclopaedia in the thirteenth century. This is what he said about what went on at a feast in a large castle hall.

'At feasts, first the meat is prepared and shown to everyone. Benches, tables and stools are put out, and cloths and towels made ready. Guests sit with the lord at their own table. When knives, spoons and salt are laid out, drink and bread and other dishes are brought. The guests enjoy the sound of lutes and harps. Then wine and dishes of meat are brought. Finally fruit and spices appear. When they have eaten, the cloths and trestle-tables are taken away. Guests wash and wipe their hands. Grace is said and people thank the lord. Then for gladness and comfort more drink is brought.'

Bartholomew the Englishman, The Nature of Things, about 1260

Source C

This picture of a dinner was drawn in the late thirteenth century to tell a story about good and evil but we can use it as a source of information about castle feasts.

Source D

The food served was one way of impressing guests. Peacocks and swans were tough to eat but looked good on the table. This is a medieval recipe.

'Take a peacock, break his neck and cut his throat. Flay him (i.e. take off the skin with the feathers attached); gut him like a hen; keep the bone of the neck; then roast him. Put the bone back into the neck; let him cool and then bind the skin and feathers back around the body and add the tail. Serve him as if he were alive.'

Unknown writer, about 1450

---

1 What can you learn from Source C about
♦ food eaten
♦ clothes worn
♦ castle architecture
♦ wall decoration (shown round the edge)
♦ what happened at dinner
♦ the actions the artist thought were good
♦ the actions the artist thought were bad?

2 You have been asked to write a realistic play about life in a medieval castle. You need to decide which aspects of castle life to show. Using the information and sources in this unit decide:
♦ how long a period of time the play should cover;
♦ which parts of the castle should be shown;
♦ which characters you will include;
♦ the main actions to be shown in the play;
♦ what are the main difficulties in presenting a realistic play about life in a medieval castle?

7

Uniting the kingdoms?

William the Conqueror was the first king of England who tried to rule other parts of the British Isles. Castles were used as signs of English power in Ireland, Scotland and Wales, but they were not the only castles built in those places.

What can castles tell us about English imperialism between 1066 and 1550?

The kingdoms of Britain

The kingdom of England, which William took in 1066, was smaller than England is today. Beyond the River Humber in the north lay areas ruled by great earls. In Wales the princes ruled. Ireland was split into several kingdoms. The king of Scotland ruled the Central Lowlands but the Highlands were governed by chieftains of the clans. The king of Norway ruled the Western Isles till 1266 and kept control of Orkney and Shetland for much longer. The British Isles formed a patchwork of different lands and rulers.

William was also Duke of Normandy. From a heartland of Normandy and southern England the influence of the kings of England spread outwards to Ireland, Scotland and Wales and to other parts of France. Sometimes this happened peacefully by marriage, at other times violently by the sword. Occasionally the king even fought his own barons, as happened in Ireland in 1172.

The history of these lands in the later Middle Ages is a complex story of victories and defeats on all sides, but gradually England emerged as the strongest kingdom. Even so, by 1550 only Wales and a small part of Ireland were firmly under English control.

Building the castles

Wherever lords ruled, castles were built. The kings of England and Scotland built royal castles; so too, did the Irish kings and Welsh princes. Great nobles built their own strongholds. Depending upon their wealth, their castles were built according to the fashions of the day. After successful military campaigns, the English kings and barons built their castles in other parts of the British Isles. They were often attacked but most survive to provide us with clues about the ways castles were used in attempts to unite the British Isles under the kings of England.

SOURCE A

'The key to Scotland'. Stirling Castle belonged to the kings of Scotland. It controlled the route to the Scottish Highlands. Near here Edward II was defeated at Bannockburn in 1314.

SOURCE B

Duart Castle, Isle of Mull, is still the home of Clan Maclean. It has a thirteenth-century keep with later additions.

Castles were built by kings and powerful lords who ruled lands in various areas of the British Isles.

- What reasons did they have for building castles? Did the English kings have different reasons to the other rulers?

SOURCE C

In Ireland Trim Castle, County Meath, was built on the River Boyne in about 1230 to protect the Pale, where the English ruled, from attack. It has a large bailey which protected the English soldiers camping there.

Caernarfon Castle – a case study in imperialism

When William was defeating Harold at Hastings, Wales was ruled by Welsh princes. In 1276 the last native Prince of Wales, Llywelyn the Last, fought against Edward I. Although defeated he fought again in 1282. This time Edward built several large castles around Llywelyn's mountainous heartland of Gwynedd. North Wales still has the most spectacular concentration of castles in the British Isles. At Caernarfon Edward built a town for the English and a magnificent royal castle intended for his son, Edward, whom he made the first English Prince of Wales in 1301.

Caernarfon became a sign of English rule in Wales. In 1294 it was captured by Madog ap Llywelyn, a cousin of the last Welsh prince. In 1403 and 1404 it was attacked by the Welsh leader Owain Glyndwr in the last attempt by the Welsh to drive out the English. He failed.

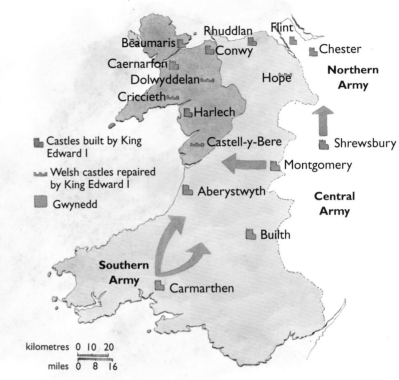

SOURCE D

A modern map showing Edward's campaign against Llywelyn in 1282–83 and the castles that were then built in north Wales.

SOURCE E

Dolbadarn Castle was built in the early thirteenth century by the Welsh prince Llywelyn the Great.

● *How does it differ from Caernarfon Castle?*

SOURCE F

The Eagle Tower of Caernarfon Castle seen from the Menai Straits. The square-sided tower and bands of stone copy the walls at Constantinople, capital of the Roman Empire of the east. The stone eagles on the turrets symbolise Roman imperialism. Edward wanted to impress the Welsh as an imperial ruler.

SOURCE G

This display in Harlech Castle tells of Edward's second campaign.

● *Do you think the reaction of people who read the left-hand side, written in Welsh, will be the same as those reading the right-hand side, written in English?*

SOURCE H

Edward also built a new town at Caernarfon. Its walls are still intact and are over 700 metres long. Until 1485 only English settlers were allowed to live and trade inside the walls.

---

1 Why do you think Edward I built castles around Gwynedd?

2 Which one of these statements do you think best explains why Edward I built Caernarfon Castle?

a to protect the Menai Straits

b as a stronghold to govern north Wales

c to deter the Welsh from future uprisings

d to spread Englishness into Gwynedd

e as the symbol of an emperor building an empire

3 Discuss your choices with each other. How much do you agree? How would a visit to Caernarfon Castle help you in answering this question?

Why did castles decline?

In western Europe cannon were first used in the early fourteenth century. Cannon-balls could knock down the strongest walls. Castle building ended in the mid-sixteenth century. How were the two developments linked?

Did castles decline because cannon came into use?

When Herstmonceux Castle was being built, some castles had already become ruins. Instead of moving around the countryside, the great lords tended to establish their homes in one of their main castles, which they then made more comfortable to live in. By the time that iron cannon-balls were introduced in the middle of the fifteenth century, styles of fighting had changed. More battles took place in the open countryside than around castle walls. It is a popular idea that because castles declined *after* gunpowder came into widespread use, the decline in castles was *caused* by the development of cannon. As you will see from the sources in this chapter, the reasons for the decline of castles are complicated. Your task is to consider some of the evidence and decide why castles declined and whether the use of gunpowder was the most important reason.

Source A

A fifteenth-century drawing of cannon at a siege.

SOURCE B

A popular book on castles suggests there were many reasons for the decline of castles.

'It was impossible that the standard set by Edward I's castles in North Wales could have been kept up. They were never fully used and were too expensive to garrison. The development of great siege cannon is only one small part of a complicated process of change. Privacy and luxury became more important than defence.'

M. Prestwick, Castles, A History & Guide, 1980

SOURCE C

Early cannon were not always effective. They could also be very unreliable.

'In 1460 King James II of Scotland besieged the castle of Roxburgh in Northumberland and on St Lawrence Day before he had heard Mass he would have fired a great gun to shoot the castle, but the chamber of the gun blew up and slew him.'

Anon, An English Chronicle written before 1471

SOURCE D ▲

Herstmonceux Castle in Sussex was built by the king's treasurer in the 1440s. This was over a century after cannon had first been used. Castles built at this time were more like stately homes than fortresses.

● What features tell you that it was built more for luxury than for defence? Are there any real defensive features?

SOURCE E ▶

Deal Castle was built in the 1530s by Henry VIII as part of a plan to prevent a French attack on the south coast. It was built nearly a century later than Herstmonceux Castle.

● How can you tell it was designed more for defence than for luxury?

Castles today

Most castles today lie in ruins. There is no longer a need to defend land as in the Middle Ages, and because people want to live in greater comfort, medieval castles which were built more for defence than for luxury have been allowed to decay. In a few cases, however, families still live in them.

How has living in a castle changed since the Middle Ages?

'Slighting' the castles

Most castles were not destroyed in the Middle Ages but in the 1640s and 1650s after the English Civil War, when they were 'slighted' – or damaged – so they could no longer be defended. Some castles had already been converted into stately homes. Kenilworth is a very good example.

The oldest inhabited castle in England

Since 1153 Berkeley Castle in Gloucestershire has been one of the homes of the Berkeley family. Today it is visited by over 50,000 tourists each year. Many come to see where King Edward II was murdered and how a medieval castle has been converted into a modern home. What changes have taken place there?

SOURCE A

Berkeley Castle from the air. You can see the shell keep, built between 1153 and 1156, with its outer bailey wall. The buildings against the wall are mostly fourteenth century.

● How have the castle buildings been changed since the mid-twelfth century to make them more comfortable?

SOURCE B

Mr and Mrs Berkeley and their two sons – the present owners of Berkeley Castle.

SOURCE C

The Great Hall at Berkeley Castle was built in about 1340. The roof was rebuilt in 1497.

- *How different is the Great Hall today from how it might have looked in 1497?*

- *The Great Hall is often used by local organisations for special events and dinners. Why do you think they choose this historic room?*

SOURCE D

From 1420 to 1421 Elizabeth Berkeley, Countess of Warwick, ran the household because her husband Richard was away serving the king. Her steward kept very careful accounts, including a list of the people in the household, which we can compare with today's workers at the castle.

1420–21

The Countess
Three daughters
Six ladies-in-waiting
Three ladies' maids
Nine gentlemen
Two advisers to the Countess
Five superior servants
Fifteen grooms and lesser servants
Eleven unnamed lesser servants

Today

Resident
The four members of the Berkeley family –
(September to April)
The custodian and his wife
Non-resident
Permanent:
Two office staff
Three gardeners
Three cleaners
Temporary (April to September):
Five workers in the ticket office and shop
Ten workers in the tea room
Sixteen guides

- Have the jobs at Berkeley changed very greatly?

---

1 Use all the sources carefully to make a list of all the changes at Berkeley Castle since the Middle Ages. Are they all equally important?

2 Make a list of all the things that have not changed during that time.

3 Do you think the visitors come to see the changes or the continuities in Berkeley Castle?

4 'Castles are no longer important because we have progressed since the Middle Ages.'
Do you agree?

The nave of Durham Cathedral

William the Conqueror built new churches, just as he built
castles, to show the English they had a new king. By 1100 over
thirty great churches were being built or rebuilt. No great
Saxon church survived this change. These early Norman
churches were themselves rebuilt later. At Durham only the
nave of the cathedral survives of the original Norman church
built between 1100 and 1130, but it remains a very good
example of *Romanesque* architecture.

Salisbury Cathedral

At the end of the twelfth century another style of architecture
came from France. Over seventy-five great churches were
rebuilt in the new Gothic style called *Early English*. They were
much taller than the Norman buildings, with pointed arches
and slender graceful pillars. They had larger windows and
seemed to soar up towards heaven. Such designs were made
possible by the use of new building techniques such as flying
buttresses and rib vaulting. Salisbury Cathedral was built from
new in thirty years after 1220 although the spire was not added
till the end of the next century.

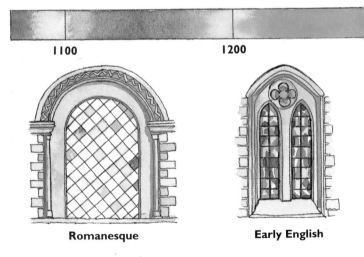

1100   1200

Romanesque   **Early English**

Most great churches are a mixture of architectural styles
because each time they were altered the latest style was

churches

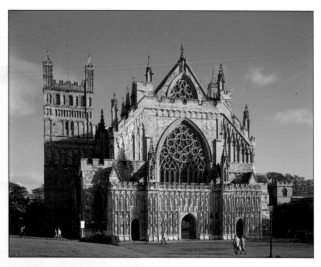

West front of Exeter Cathedral

By the middle of the thirteenth century the Early English style had become more elaborate and is called the *Decorated* style. The designers covered every available wooden or stone surface with intricate carvings. Exeter Cathedral shows this ornate style. Many great churches were rebuilt in the next century in this style before the Black Death reduced the wealth of the churches.

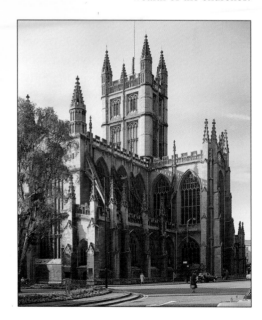

Bath Abbey

In the fifteenth and early sixteenth centuries the Gothic style developed further into the *Perpendicular* style. The strong vertical lines in the windows and panelling give this style its name. The roofs are often supported by intricate fan vaulting. Many great churches had new towers added in these years. Bath Abbey was completely rebuilt in this style just before the dissolution of the monasteries.

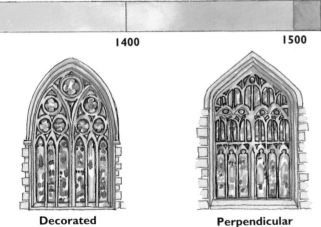

1400   1500

Decorated   **Perpendicular**

used. If we know about these styles we can work out how the great churches changed over the centuries.

10 Centres of prayer and power

Most cathedrals in use today were either built or greatly rebuilt between 1066 and 1540. From them we can learn about the importance of the Church at that time.

Why were cathedrals and monasteries important in the later Middle Ages?

Political importance

Cathedrals were built to rule dioceses. They still look powerful today. Their walls have battlements; their towers look like keeps. Many were built on prominent sites. Both castles and cathedrals represented the power of the rich. Ordinary people, who were usually kept out, had their own parish churches to meet their religious needs.

William the Conqueror knew the importance of churches as well as castles in controlling people's lives. From 1070 his new Archbishop of Canterbury, Lanfranc, organised the rebuilding of the Saxon cathedrals. In places the site of the cathedral was moved: from Selsey to Winchester; from Dorchester near Oxford to Lincoln. Medieval rulers were crowned in a cathedral (Source A). By the fifteenth century fifty-two abbots and eighteen bishops sat in the House of Lords. Not surprisingly, in times of war, cathedrals and abbeys became targets for attack.

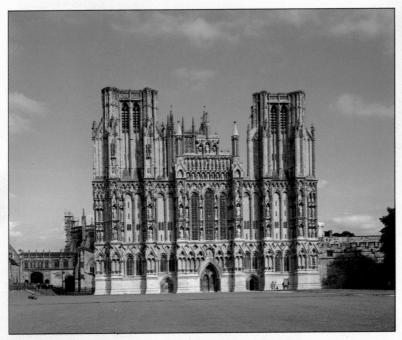

SOURCE A ▲

The coronation chair in Westminster Abbey was made in about 1300. It is still used at the coronation of the monarch.

- *Why was it important to have a coronation in an abbey or cathedral?*

◄ SOURCE B

Wells Cathedral, the west front.

Religious organisation

A cathedral is a church which contains the chair or *cathedra* of a bishop. From there he rules his diocese. Until Henry VIII closed the monasteries, there were two types of cathedral in the Middle Ages – secular cathedrals and monastic cathedrals. In a secular cathedral a group of clergy called canons, who were under the authority of the dean, worshipped and prayed on behalf of the outside world.

This is a modern artist's drawing showing the clergy who were involved in the work of a secular cathedral in about 1500.

Secular cathedrals

The canons usually lived in houses near the cathedral but although the clergy of a secular cathedral were not as separated from the community as the monks, there was still a wall surrounding the cathedral, the church lands and the homes of the clergy. The gates were open by day to receive visitors but closed at night. This enclosed area was called the cathedral close and can still be seen today in places like Wells.

Source C ►

Vicars' Close, Wells.

37

Monastic cathedrals

In monastic cathedrals, monks did the work of the canons and the bishop was also an abbot. The monks were organised by a prior and lived in a closed community. The cathedral was built in the monastery grounds which were enclosed by a wall. Although many of their buildings were destroyed when the monasteries were closed, some still survive. Worcester is a good example (Source D). When Henry VIII closed the monasteries these monks became canons and there was no longer any difference between the monastic and secular cathedrals.

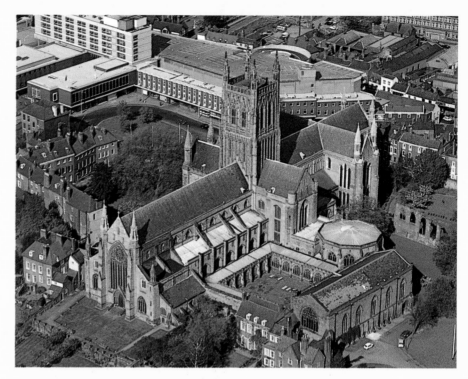

Worcester Cathedral is unusual because the monastic buildings still survive around the cloister. It gives a good impression of what a medieval monastery looked like. You can compare this with some of the ruins shown in later chapters.

Economic importance

Cathedrals and monasteries were important in the daily lives of ordinary people because the bishops and abbots were their landlords and owned nearly a third of the land of England and Wales. Just like the king or the nobles, the bishops controlled large estates. They granted land to peasants and received rent and work in return. Bishops held courts and passed laws relating to religion. Many bishops were the sons of kings and nobles and were, themselves, extremely powerful people.

SOURCE E

Cathedrals and monasteries kept careful records of their estates. Historians have used them to build up pictures of life on the medieval manor. In 1183 the Bishop of Durham had a survey made of his nearby manor of Boldon. This is part of it.

'In Boldon there are 22 villeins, every one of whom holds 60 acres of land and pays 2s 6d [12½p] of corn tax and 16 pence [7p] of annual tax and 5 wagonloads of wood and 2 hens and 10 eggs, and works throughout the whole year 3 days in the week, except Easter and Whitsun week and 13 days at Christmas-tide, and in his works he does in the autumn 4 boondays of reaping with his entire household, except the housewife.'

Boldon Book, 1183

SOURCE F

This extract illustrates another side of the economic importance of monasteries. In this charter a corrody (pension) is granted to two tenants from a manor belonging to Lacock Abbey in Wiltshire. The tenants received all this in return for a payment to the nunnery at Lacock.

'Notification by Beatrice, abbess of Lacock, that she is bound to Walter, son of the priest of Woodmancote and Mabel his wife to provide them a suitable house in Lacock and to keep it in repair and roof it at her own cost as long as they shall live. She is also bound to provide each day two white loaves and two gallons of nuns' beer, and a dish of food from her kitchen. And 6s [30p] a year for their clothes and other things and four cartloads of wood a year.'

Lacock Abbey Cartulary, 1257–83

● Do you think Walter and Mabel felt the same way towards the nuns at Lacock as the villeins of Boldon did towards the Bishop of Durham?

Art and technology

Cathedrals and monasteries were centres of both prayer and power. They were also masterpieces of art and architecture, of technology and engineering as medieval masons became ever bolder in overcoming problems of design. What they built often survives to help us understand the later Middle Ages better.

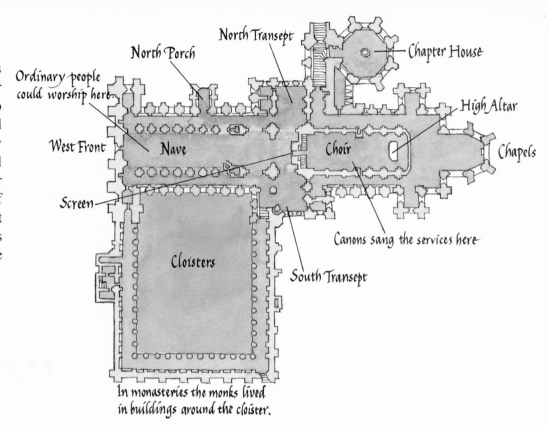

North Transept

North Porch

Chapter House

Ordinary people could worship here

West Front

Nave

High Altar

Choir

Chapels

Screen

Canons sang the services here

Cloisters

South Transept

In monasteries the monks lived in buildings around the cloister.

SOURCE G

This plan view, based on Wells Cathedral, shows the main areas where the worship and work of the medieval cathedral were carried out. The rood screen separated the nave, which the ordinary townspeople were allowed to enter, from the rest of the cathedral which was used by the clergy for their religious services. The choir was where they sang and prayed at regular times throughout the day.

The sanctuary is the holy place where Mass was celebrated every day at the high altar. There were also side chapels and shrines where services were held and where rich families could pay for Mass to be chanted for their souls to go to heaven. Poor people who could not afford such services simply visited the cathedral shrines which often contained relics of saints.

---

1 There are several special words in this unit linked to cathedrals and monasteries. How many of these can you explain without re-reading the text:
Secular cathedral, monastic cathedral, *cathedra*, **bishop, diocese, canon, dean, abbot, monk, prior.**

2 Copy this list and the table below:
a Rulers in the Middle Ages
b Ordinary people in the Middle Ages
c Poor people in the Middle Ages
d Ourselves today

	a	b	c	d
Worship and prayer				
Power and authority				
Alms and hospitality				
Art and technology				

Using the information in this chapter put a tick in one or more of the boxes to show the importance of cathedrals and monasteries for the four different types of people.
Work in a group of four. Each choose a different letter: **a, b, c** or **d**. Explain to the rest of your group why cathedrals and abbeys were important for the type of person you have chosen.
When each of you has explained, suggest reasons why there is no simple answer to the question at the start of the unit.

Work, prayer and study?

Monks and nuns attended eight church services every day and, in between, their lives were filled with work and study. They were supposed to live according to strict rules but they were often criticised for failing to do so.

What was life like for monks and nuns?

Were the monks and nuns different?

Monks and nuns had to make a solemn promise or profession. This made them different from the rest of the population.

Monks and nuns had to promise these things:

- stability – to remain in the same monastery for the rest of their lives;

- conversion of life – to remain poor and never to marry;

- obedience – to obey their superiors and God.

Any male from a free peasant family or higher could become a monk, but nuns were nearly all from richer families who found it cheaper to give a daughter to a nunnery than provide her with a marriage dowry.

How many monks and nuns were there?

Year	Monks and nuns	Religious houses
1066	1000	60
1350	18000	1000
1535	10000	850

SOURCE A

A medieval painting of nuns in the choir.

What was daily life like?

Each day had a regular pattern based on the eight services, but the times changed. One reason was that the day started at sunrise and ended at sunset, so there was less time in winter for work and reading. The table below shows a typical summer's day. Copy it into your books. Look at the drawing of Tintern Abbey on pages 44–45 and in the third column write in where the activity took place. This will show you how the parts of the monastery were used.

SOURCE B

In 1066 all the monks and nuns were meant to follow the rules written by St Benedict. They worshipped seven times during the day and once at night. The rest of their day was filled with work.

'Idleness is the enemy of the soul. For this reason the brothers should be occupied at certain times in manual labour and at other times in sacred reading.'

Rule of St Benedict, Chapter 48

Time	Activity	Place
Shortly after midnight	Matins	
	Sleep	
Sunrise	Lauds and Prime	
	Chapter Meeting	
Mid-morning	Terce and Mass	
	Work or reading	
	Sext	
Midday	Dinner	
	Siesta or reading	
Early afternoon	Nones	
	Work	
Evening	Vespers	
	Supper	
	Reading	
Sunset	Compline	
	Sleep	

New religious orders

Many people gave land and money to the monks and nuns so they would pray for them when they died. This made many monasteries very rich and by 1100 a new religious order – the Cistercians – had been formed to try to bring simplicity back into monastic life. They settled in the countryside away from the towns. Another new order – the Gilbertines – allowed monks and nuns to live in double monasteries without meeting. Their church was divided down the middle!

Unlike monks or nuns, friars travelled round preaching. The idea came from St Francis of Assisi, and the friars first arrived in England in the 1220s. They owned no land but relied on charity. They became popular preachers but, as time went on, many people thought they were more interested in collecting money than in saving souls.

41

One of the founders of the Cistercians was a monk called St Bernard of Clairvaux. This is part of his criticism of existing monasteries.

'Being a monk myself, I ask other monks, "You say you are poor, why do you need gold in a holy place?" The sight of these fancy decorated churches encourages visitors to give money rather than to pray.'

St Bernard of Clairvaux, *Apologia*, early twelfth century

The strictest reforming order was the Carthusian order which was founded at La Grande Chartreuse in the French Alps in 1084. Only a few monasteries followed the Carthusian rules. This description of life in a Carthusian monastery shows how strict they were.

'There were thirteen monks. They all have cells of their own round the cloister where they work, sleep and eat. On Sunday they receive their food for the week, that is bread and vegetables which is cooked by each of them in his own quarters. Fish and cheese they use on Sundays and holy days. They almost never speak, for if anything necessary is wanted, it is got by sign. They are clad in hair shirts next to their skin, and the rest of their garments are very poor.'

Description of La Grande Chartreuse by Gilbert of Nugent about 1100

The remains of Mount Grace Priory in north Yorkshire shows how the Carthusian monks were different. Visitors were kept out of the monastic cloister; instead they stayed in the guest house, now the mansion. The church was small because the monks seldom met together. The life of a Carthusian monk was different from that of other orders and the remains of Carthusian monasteries show this clearly. There was no refectory or dormitory. Instead each monk lived in his own cell – a small two-roomed house with a garden which he tended himself. For much of the day he studied, worked and ate alone. In a Carthusian monastery the church and communal buildings were small and simple but the cloister was large because all the cells were arranged around it.

People in the monastery

Many monks and nuns had special jobs. The prior was second to the abbot and had to keep order. The sacristan made sure the church was ready for the services. New monks or nuns were looked after by the novice master.

- Can you work out what these people did: cellarer, kitchener, infirmarer, hospitaller?

Until the fourteenth century Cistercian monasteries had lay brothers (servants who lived in the monasteries) to do the manual tasks, but they were gradually replaced by hired servants as in other monasteries. At Glastonbury in 1190 sixty-five monks employed eighty-three servants. At St Radegunde's in Cambridge there were only twelve nuns in 1450 but they employed three chaplains, three male and four female domestic servants and six male farm servants. Normally there were stewards, who looked after the monasteries' lands, and bailiffs who collected the rents.

Learning and letters

Monasteries were centres of study and learning in the Middle Ages. Some monks were skilled in writing or illuminating manuscripts written on parchment or vellum. Illumination is the term which describes the brilliantly coloured ornate decorations which were added to the manuscript after the writing had been done.

SOURCE G

A medieval manuscript. Holes are sometimes made by accident during the preparation of parchment. The scribe has carefully written his text around the hole in this late twelfth–century manuscript made probably at Winchcombe Abbey in Gloucestershire.

SOURCE H

A scribe.

Life in a monastery

SOURCE I

Look at this drawing of Tintern,
a Cistercian abbey in south Wales, as it might
have looked in 1500. Study it carefully to work out
where the monks spent the different parts of their day.

● *Many monastic sites now have display boards to explain to visitors what happened in the monastery.*
As a class, plan display boards for the different parts of Tintern Abbey using the information in this unit.
Be sure to include illustrations to make it interesting.

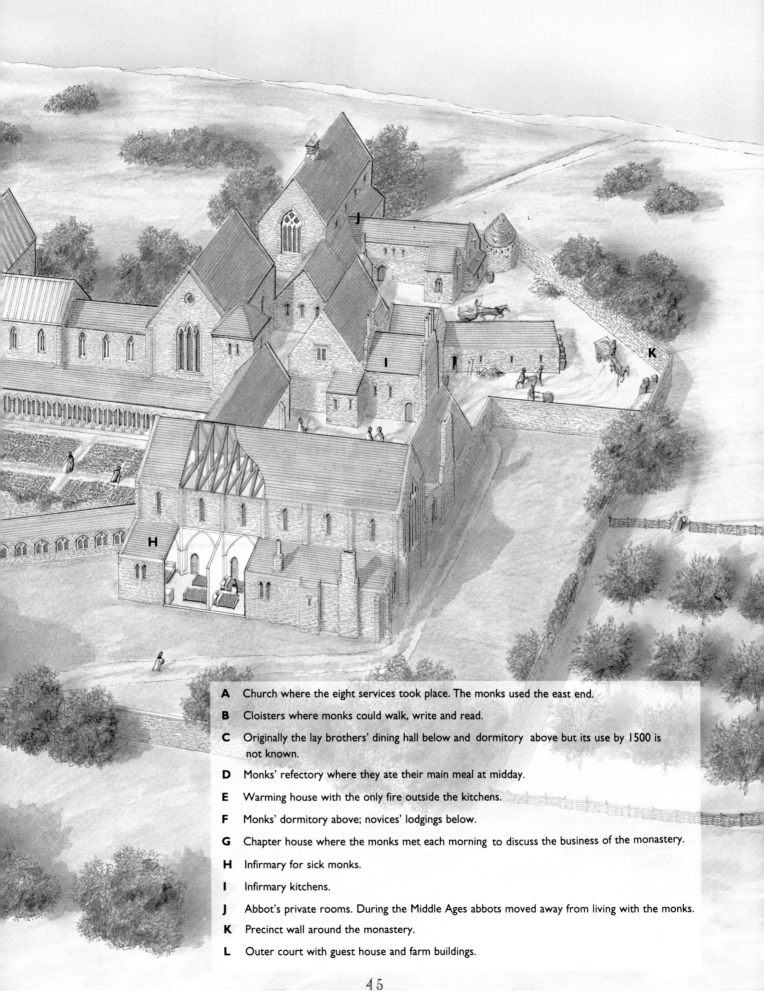

A Church where the eight services took place. The monks used the east end.

B Cloisters where monks could walk, write and read.

C Originally the lay brothers' dining hall below and dormitory above but its use by 1500 is not known.

D Monks' refectory where they ate their main meal at midday.

E Warming house with the only fire outside the kitchens.

F Monks' dormitory above; novices' lodgings below.

G Chapter house where the monks met each morning to discuss the business of the monastery.

H Infirmary for sick monks.

I Infirmary kitchens.

J Abbot's private rooms. During the Middle Ages abbots moved away from living with the monks.

K Precinct wall around the monastery.

L Outer court with guest house and farm buildings.

45

Communal life

The remains of monasteries can tell us much but not everything about life in them. Other sources are needed to make the empty walls live again with monks and nuns. They weren't always very holy!

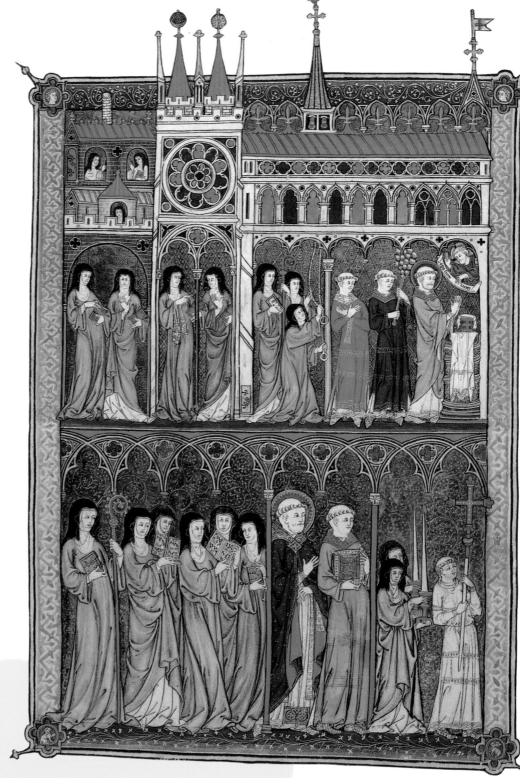

SOURCE J

Nuns on their way to prayer in about 1300. They are led by their chaplains who were needed to say Mass.

SOURCE K

A description of the work of the nuns at Kington St Michael in Wiltshire was written by a seventeenth-century historian, John Aubrey, who visited the site a hundred and fifty years after the nunnery was closed.

'There young maids were brought up where they had examples of piety and humility, modesty and obedience to imitate. Here they learned needlework, the art of confectionery, surgery, writing and drawing. This was a fine way of bringing up young women.'

John Aubrey, 1696

● John Aubrey was obviously biased in favour of the closed nunnery. Does this make his description unreliable?

46

The Holy Blood of Hailes – a case study

Hailes Abbey was a Cistercian monastery founded in 1245 at the foot of the Cotswold Hills in Gloucestershire. In 1270 it was given a small glass phial said to contain the blood of Christ from the cross. Hailes became one of the most important centres of pilgrimage in England. Pilgrims were encouraged to visit it by the pope. People, then and since, thought it was a fake. These sources have been chosen to show you some of the problems faced by modern historians in trying to decide the real importance of the Holy Blood of Hailes.

It will help you if you try to separate fact from opinion and try to work out the motives of the different writers. The two questions below should help you to come to your own conclusions but do not be surprised if your friends have other ideas!

SOURCE H

A monk at Hailes describes how the blood was found by a nephew of Henry III. His father, who was the Earl of Cornwall, also had the title 'King of the Romans'.

'Edmund, the young son of Richard King of the Romans, [founder of Hailes] discovered the Holy Blood amongst precious relics in a secret room, whilst playing in a castle in Germany.'

From *The Annals of Hailes*, thirteenth century

A modern artists impression of Hailes Abbey and the surrounding countryside.

SOURCE I

This is the only detailed account to survive describing what happened at the shrine. It was written after the monastery had been closed.

'The priest showed the blood in a cabinet of crystal both sides of which seemed alike, yet one side was thicker than the other. Until the pilgrim had paid for as many masses as the priest thought were needed, the side with the thicker crystal was shown, so nothing could be seen. When he had paid to the priest's satisfaction the thin side was shown and to his great joy he saw the blood.'

Anonymous, about 1540

SOURCE J

The blood was examined just before the monastery closed.

'We have examined the supposed relic called the Blood of Hailes and judged it to be an oily, coloured gum which appears red in the glass but when taken out shines yellow like false gold.'

Certificate of the king's commissioners, October 1538

SOURCE K

Some people said that it was duck's blood, others that it was honey. These stories were used later by Protestant historians to attack the Roman Catholic Church, but they may not provide reliable evidence.

'The relic may not have been what it was supposed to be but we cannot trust the sensational statements made at the time of the Dissolution, and afterwards, as to what its nature really was.'

The archaeologist who first excavated Hailes Abbey, W. St Clair Baddeley, 1908

---

1 What are the main problems in trying to decide what was in the phial?

2 What do you think is more useful for us today – to find out what was in the phial or to find out why people in the Middle Ages thought it was important?

13

'Bare ruin'd choirs'

No new medieval cathedral or monastery was built after the Black Death in 1348–49. Just two hundred years later all the monasteries were closed on the orders of King Henry VIII and his chief minister Thomas Cromwell. Historians call this the dissolution of the monasteries. This was one of the most important events in English history.

Why were the monasteries and nunneries closed and what were the results?

Were the monks and nuns enemies of the king?

In 1535 Henry VIII made himself head of the Church in England. Henry feared that the monks and nuns might try to lead the English Church back to the Pope, but in fact very few of them protested at the dissolution. Some Carthusian monks and a handful of abbots and other religious leaders were executed for objecting. So too were the leaders of an uprising in 1536 in the north of England called the Pilgrimage of Grace, which tried to stop the changes.

SOURCE A

Visitation and Surrender of Syon Nunnery to the Commissioners, 1539, *which was painted in the nineteenth century.*

Were the monks and nuns behaving badly?

In 1535 Thomas Cromwell started to send commissioners round the religious houses to find reasons to close them. They concentrated on finding monks and nuns who were not living holy lives. Study the following reports. Why do you think historians still argue about whether they can be trusted?

SOURCE B

Langdon monastery in Kent was visited in 1535.

'I myself went alone to the abbot's lodging which lies next to the fields and wood. I spent a good time knocking at the abbot's door but no person appeared except the abbot's little dog which barked. Then I found a small pole-axe behind the door and with it I dashed the abbot's door in pieces, and took it around the house with me, for the abbot is a dangerous, desperate knave. But in the end his whore, alias his gentlewoman, stirred herself and after I had questioned her, I took her to Dover to the mayor to put her in prison for eight days, and I brought holy father abbot to Canterbury and here I will leave him in prison.'

Letter from Dr Richard Layton to Thomas Cromwell, 1535

EARL OF ESSEX.

SOURCE D

Thomas Cromwell.

- What do you think was the writer's intention in making this report about the abbot of Langdon monastery?

SOURCE C

Tintern Abbey.

SOURCE E

Catesby nunnery in Northamptonshire was visited the following year.

'The prioress is a wise and very religious woman with nine nuns as religious, devout and obedient as we have seen in times past, or are likely to see.'

Letter from George Gifford to Henry VIII, 1536

- When he read this, Henry accused Gifford of having been bribed. Why might he have accused him?

Did Henry need the monasteries' money?

Henry was spending more than he could afford on royal palaces and foreign wars. His annual income was £100,000. In 1535 he organised a survey of the wealth of the monasteries and found their income was £160,000 from land and gifts. All this became his by 1540 after the last monasteries had been closed.

What were the results of the dissolution?

All the monks and nuns were given annual pensions. Some abbots and priors became rich enough to buy country estates. Twenty of them became bishops and continued to live comfortable lives. Most monks and many friars became parish or family priests, but many nuns just returned to their families. Ten years later the law was changed to allow them to marry.

The power of the Church became much less and people stopped going on pilgrimages. Although some monastic churches became parish churches, most were quickly destroyed. Lands were soon sold to rich local people and to the officials who had helped in the dissolution. Beautiful architecture, books, stained glass, metalwork and jewellery were lost. But the number of cathedrals increased because Henry made six monasteries into new cathedrals.

The profit to the King from the dissolution was not as great as may be imagined. Because of the heavy cost of the war against France, together with the burden of paying pensions, the seizure of religious property did not add greatly to the wealth of the crown in the long term.

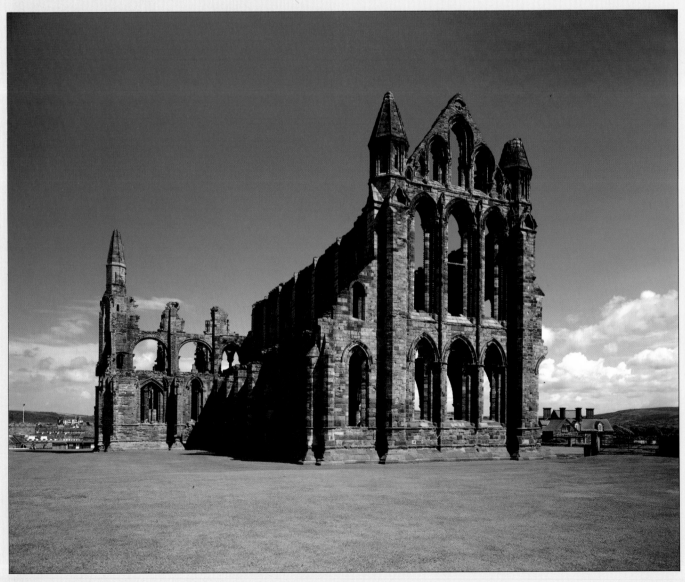

SOURCE F

Whitby Abbey.

SOURCE G

Some ruins became romantic places to visit. William Shakespeare later described them as 'bare ruin'd choirs where late the sweet birds sang'. The picture above is a detail of a Romantic painting of Kirkstall Abbey, Leeds, made by J.M.W. Turner in the early nineteenth century.

1 The dissolution was a religious event, but its causes were not only religious. They were also economic and political. Find examples of each of these three types of cause. Decide which type was most important.

2 Some of the results of the dissolution were planned, some were not. Find examples of both types of result. Would you say that the dissolution all went according to plan?

14

Downside Abbey

You can find medieval monasteries and cathedrals surviving today in many forms. Today there are over 1,000 monks and nuns in Britain living in nearly one hundred monastic houses. One of the largest is the Roman Catholic Benedictine Abbey of Downside near Bath in Somerset. A visit there can help us compare life in a monastery today with that in the Middle Ages.

What are the similarities and differences between life in a medieval monastery and life in a modern monastery?

'In touch with the tradition of the past'

Father Philip Jebb, the Prior of Downside, is proud of the house's history because it has an unbroken link with medieval monasteries. In 1607 the last surviving monk from Westminster Abbey blessed two young Englishmen training to be monks in Rome. They joined up with other English monks in France, where many lived until the French Revolution. They then had to flee, and in 1814 finally arrived at Downside to begin building a new monastery. Just like medieval monasteries, building and rebuilding took many years. Most of the church was built by 1925 but it is still not completely finished.

The monastery today

Forty monks belong to Downside but not all of them live there; one is a chaplain in Boston, USA. At Downside there is still an abbot, a cellarer (called the bursar), hospitaller (or guestmaster), infirmarer, sacristan and novicemaster. These roles were also carried out in the Middle Ages.

Prayer and study are still very important. So too are pilgrims who visit the shrine of Oliver Plunkett, which is at Downside. He was the last person in England to be hung, drawn and quartered for his Roman Catholic beliefs. However, most of the income comes from Downside School, a boarding school for boys, where many of the monks teach. The monks also own a farm and publish books. Their library has 100,000 books and is world famous.

The monastery today is a large organisation. So were medieval monasteries. From the information in this unit, do you think monastic life changed or is it still very similar?

Father Philip Jebb, Prior of Downside Abbey.

1 Make two lists: one of changes and one of continuities between medieval monasteries and Downside Abbey today. Compare your list with those made by the rest of the class.

2 Do you think that the changes mean the lives of monks today are better than those of monks and nuns in the Middle Ages?

3 Do you think Father Philip Jebb would think the things that have not changed are more important than the things that have changed? Would you agree with him?

The daily routine at Downside:

Time	Activity
6.30 a.m.	Matins
	Breakfast (self-service)
8.45 a.m.	Mass (10.00 on Sunday)
9.20 a.m.	Work at appointed tasks, e.g. teaching, study
1.00 p.m.	Midday service
1.15 p.m.	Lunch in silence listening to a monk reading aloud
2.00 p.m.	Work
4.00 p.m.	Recreation; tea and chat
5.00 p.m.	Reading and prayer
6.30 p.m.	Vespers
7.00 p.m.	Supper in silence with reading
7.30 p.m.	Recreation
8.15 p.m.	Compline
8.30 p.m.	The Greater Silence (retire to room and sleep)

● Compare this with the timetable in Unit 11. What are the similarities and differences?

SOURCE B

Downside Abbey: monastery and school.

● *Compare this photograph with the picture of Tintern Abbey in Unit 13. What similarities and differences can you see?*

15 Looking for clues

No study of castles, cathedrals or monasteries is complete without a visit. Use your visit to look for clues to bring you closer to the people who lived in the Middle Ages. This unit will help you plan your own activities to do just that.

How can a visit to a castle, cathedral or monastery help us understand more about its past?

Start by asking questions about the buildings themselves. Sometimes the site itself will help you to discover why the buildings are there but you will probably need to do further research. Use your knowledge of architectural styles or development of castle design to work out which are the earliest surviving parts of the building. This will help you to date it but you will need to check there were no earlier buildings that have completely disappeared. The number of different styles and designs will give you some clues about how the buildings were changed during the Middle Ages. Have they been deliberately destroyed, or just decayed, or even rebuilt to look like they once did? You might need to find out more from books and other sources.

The most important part of the study of castles, cathedrals and monasteries is the study of the people who lived in and used the buildings. Heraldry on coats of arms will give you some clues about the important people connected with the site. Although writing on medieval tombs and graves is in Latin you can usually read the name and date, and the effigy can sometimes help you understand what the people looked like. What sort of people do you find out about in this way? Are they only the rich and powerful; are women included? What conclusions can you draw from your answer?

The information in this book will help you work out how people in the past used the site you are visiting. Using the flow diagram, put all this into practice by designing your own activity sheet.

ENQUIRIES

ABOUT THE BUILDING
Why was it built here?
When was it first built?
What did it look like then?

ABOUT CHANGE
How did the site change in the Middle Ages?
How has it changed since?
Why did the changes take place?

ABOUT PEOPLE
Who built it or rebuilt it?
Who lived there?
Did different types of people live there?
How did they use the site?

CLUES TO THINK ABOUT

Architectural styles
Castle design
Geography of site

Architectural styles and designs
Surviving foundations
Roofless walls
Nineteenth- and twentieth-century rebuilding and repair

Tombs and graves
Heraldry and coats of arms
Fireplaces, windows, altars

DESIGNING YOUR SHEET

Can you make it attractive by
- including sketches
- making pattern borders
- word-processing?

Make a plan of the site
- to help you find your way
- to record the position of the features
- to label as you go round.

Decide whether you are going to
- write in words and sentences
- sketch
- measure
- photograph
- video
- role-play
- play medieval music on tape

PRESENTING YOUR FINDINGS

Make a folder, wall display, talk, tape
Write a play, story, song, poem
Design a guidebook for other people

HOW USEFUL WAS YOUR VISIT?

What new ideas and knowledge did you learn?
How well did you work with others?
How sure are you of your findings?
How useful do people find your presentation?

Drawing the past

When you visit the site of a castle or monastery you can often find in the guidebook or on display boards, artists' drawings of what the place might have looked like in the past. Terry Ball is the artist who produced these drawings of Lindisfarne Priory for English Heritage. What information did he need before he could draw his final reconstruction of what the Priory looked like in the Middle Ages? Think about the problems he faced and how he solved them.

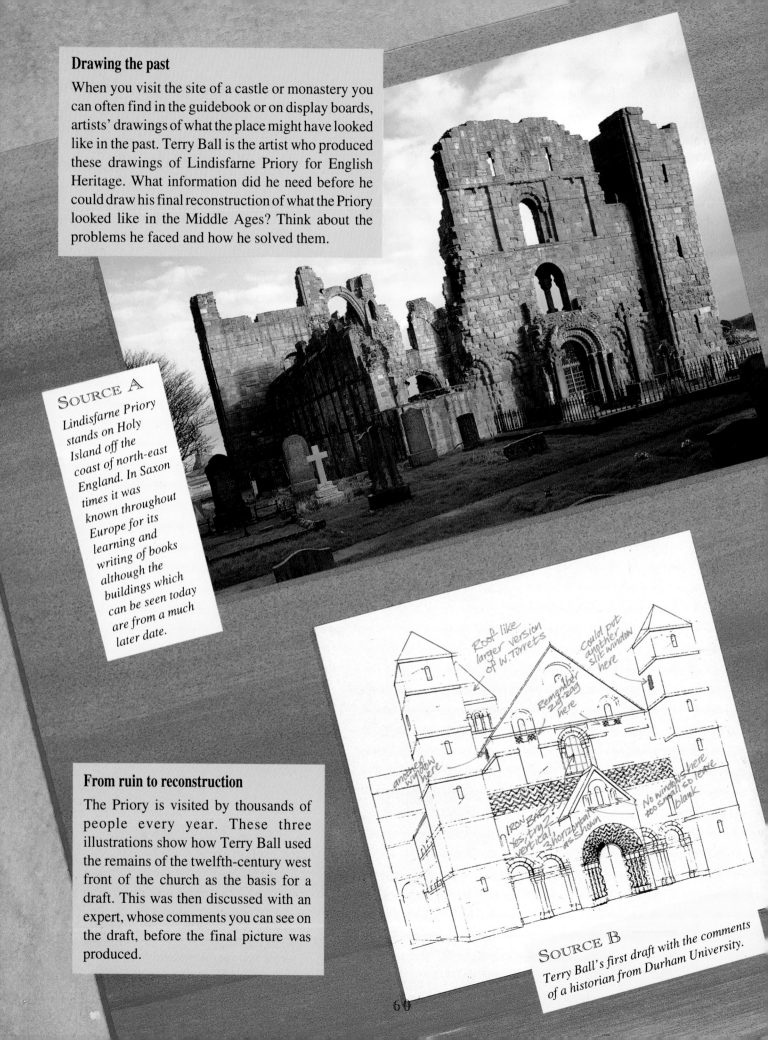

SOURCE A

Lindisfarne Priory stands on Holy Island off the coast of north-east England. In Saxon times it was known throughout Europe for its learning and writing of books although the buildings which can be seen today are from a much later date.

From ruin to reconstruction

The Priory is visited by thousands of people every year. These three illustrations show how Terry Ball used the remains of the twelfth-century west front of the church as the basis for a draft. This was then discussed with an expert, whose comments you can see on the draft, before the final picture was produced.

Roof like larger version of W. Turrets

Could put another slit window here

Remember zig-zag here

another window here

IRON BARS yes; try 2, vertical,

Shorter but as shown

No windows here too small so leave blank

SOURCE B
Terry Ball's first draft with the comments of a historian from Durham University.

60

'My main problem is lack of evidence because often so much of the building has been destroyed. That leads to another problem. In the nineteenth century, people actually rebuilt castles and some great churches to make them look medieval. Once we spot this, the different stonework usually gives it away. However, we thought that all the battlements on the Tower of London were Victorian until recently when we found a bit of the actual medieval battlements. The Victorians had made good copies!

To try to overcome these problems I study the remains of the buildings very carefully. I research all the available information about the site including written historical descriptions, modern archaeological reports, aerial photographs and old prints. When I have all the information I start by drawing outline pencil sketches and sometimes making a cardboard model to find the best viewing point. I then contact various experts such as archaeologists, university lecturers and the inspectors of English Heritage. We discuss any differences of opinion, then the final drawing is made using water colours.

I think that it is important to remind people that the finished drawing is only my opinion and not what the building actually looked like. Other people sometimes disagree with me because they have their own opinions. New findings might mean that I have to change my drawings. I am sometimes asked to redraw buildings drawn by Alan Sorrell in the 1960s. He drew marvellous pictures but we now know more about the sites than he did then.'

Terry Ball, artist working for English Heritage, 1992

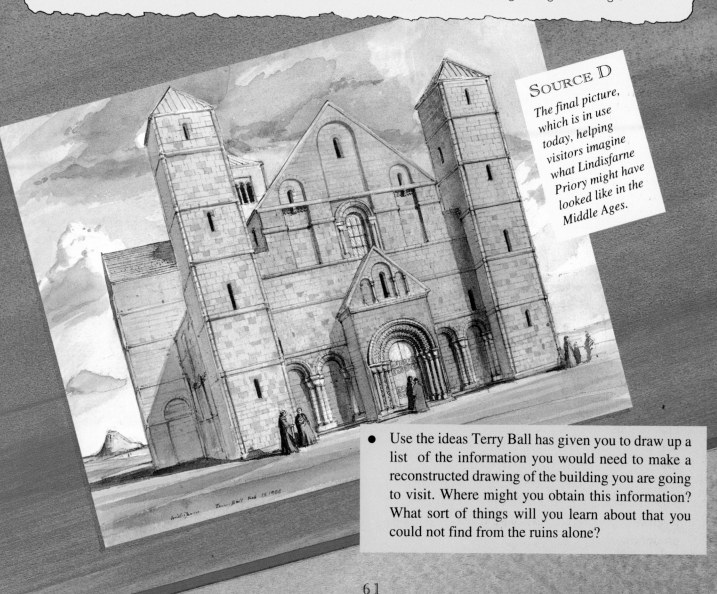

The final picture, which is in use today, helping visitors imagine what Lindisfarne Priory might have looked like in the Middle Ages.

● Use the ideas Terry Ball has given you to draw up a list of the information you would need to make a reconstructed drawing of the building you are going to visit. Where might you obtain this information? What sort of things will you learn about that you could not find from the ruins alone?

Attainment target grid

This grid is designed to indicate the varying emphases on attainment targets in the questions in each unit. It is not to be interpreted as a rigid framework, but as a simple device to help the teacher plan the study unit.

X   some focus
XX   strong focus
XXX   main focus

		AT 1 a	b	c	AT2	AT3
1	Monuments to feudalism		XX	X		XXX
2	Building castles and cathedrals	X				XXX
3	Changing castle styles	XXX				
4	'The bones of the kingdom'		XXX			
5	Keys to the land					XXX
6	Life in the castle			XXX	X	XX
7	Uniting the kingdoms?		XXX	X	X	
8	Why did castles decline?				XXX	X
9	Castles today	XXX		XX		
10	Centres of prayer and power		X	XXX		X
11	Work, prayer and study?		X	XX		XXX
12	Shrines, relics and pilgrims		XX	XXX	X	
13	'Bare ruin'd choirs'		XXX			
14	Downside Abbey	XXX			X	X
15	Looking for clues				XXX	XX

Attainment target focus

Index